1ST STEP: QUICK START GUIDE TO BUILDING YOUR SUCCESSFUL BUSINESS IN REAL ESTATE

Table of Contents

INTRODUCTION _____ 3

Chapter 1: The Foundation_____ 5

Chapter 2: Entity, Systems, and Accounts _____ 15

Chapter 3: Build Your Team _____ 23

Chapter 4: Documents _____ 33

Chapter 5: Strategies _____ 39

Chapter 6: The Process of the Purchase _____ 51

Chapter 7: Post Acquisition _____ 65

Chapter 8: Service/Product _____ 71

Chapter 9: Problem Solving _____ 75

Chapter 10: Finances and Tracking _____ 79

Chapter 11-Asset Protection _____ 83

Chapter 12-Fear is Fake _____ 89

Chapter 13-Take Action _____ 95

Recommend Reading List_____ 99

Copyright © 2019 Adam Johnson
All rights reserved.

IMPORTANT DISCLOSURE- PLEASE READ THIS!

The information contained in this book is for informational and educational purposes only and should not be wholly or partially relied upon without the advice of a competent professional advisor.

This book is meant as a general overview of several concepts and tools. It is critical that in your own real estate business you receive guidance from qualified and experienced CPAs, attorneys, contractors, etc. Due to laws and regulations constantly changing and that they vary from state to state, this book cannot and does not apply to any specific jurisdiction. We recommend that you verify the concepts and tools suggested in this book are appropriate in the state where you reside or chose to conduct business. Nothing herein should be construed as legal, tax, or other professional advice and should be independently verified with your professional advisors.

INTRODUCTION

My wife, Asury, and I have enveloped ourselves in learning, researching, and implementing the tools and strategies described in this book. We both come from humble beginnings and are a testament as to the possibilities gained from having the right mindset and education. We both left the security of being steady employees because our business has allowed us to work for ourselves and own our own time. Through implementing the system mentioned here within and building a reliable team, we can operate our business from anywhere in the world.

I served over 15 years in the US Army. After four years of being an investor, my wife and I realized our real estate business would allow me to leave the military and provide us the ability to be home with our children. For Asury and I, our most important resource is our time. When we began our business, we did so with the goal to be financially free and to own our time. We no longer clock in at an office to serve an employer or go into work for extended periods of training and time away from home and our family. Never again will we miss a school play, a soccer match, or a family get together because we must "go to work."

We have designed "1st Step-The Quick Start Guide to Building Your Successful Business in Real Estate" as a guide to help not only motivate young investors but also to point them in the right direction. What makes "1st Step" unique is it provides you specific instruction from the very beginning. Many real estate programs show you how to buy, flip, and sell a house. I have yet to find a program that says, "Hey, this is what you do on day one. This is how you set up this account. This is how you deal with contractors, etc."

We hope this book will put you in the right mindset and push you into searching for and enjoying a better version of your lives. I've always said, "We don't get time back. Once it's gone, it's gone forever." Use real estate as the vehicle that allows you to have more TIME with the ones you love doing the things you enjoy.

Chapter 1: The Foundation

"THERE'S NO GROWTH IN YOUR COMFORT ZONE"

We all have ambitions of doing better, providing a better life for our loved ones, spending more time with our families, and taking that vacation that we've dreamed about since we studied the history of ancient Rome in middle school. We hear the commercial on the radio that is advertising great airfare rates to Hawaii. We see the TV commercial that Sandals has an all-inclusive package for under $5,000 at a luxury resort in the Caribbean. We want to be there and we think of how amazing a life of travel and more freedom would be.

Then we wake up the next morning and get right back into our daily routine. Get up at 5:30 a.m. to make the kids some breakfast, if we have time. We leave the house by 7:30 a.m. to sit in traffic dreading the day ahead of us. We get to our workplace and we wait until the exact moment to "clock in." We work doing the same activity for hours at a time. We leave work around 5:00 p.m. to sit in rush-hour traffic. We get home around 6:00 p.m. in time to warm up leftovers from two days ago, and hopefully help the kids with their homework. Then we get the kids, and ourselves, ready for bed. We go to bed and repeat the same routine at least five days a week.

After all is said and done, what have we done for ourselves during that day? What have we done for ourselves during that week? Just about nothing. We almost certainly made no significant steps towards building *our* better life. At this point, we are merely surviving, not thriving. Many of us will perform this "routine" from the age of 16 to the age of 63. Some of us may do this even longer. That is not the kind of life that we are put on earth to live.

In the meantime, as we continue to slog our way through life with our "routine," the owner of the company we work for surely isn't working those same hours. Nope, he or she is living the life you have dreamed of. The owner is on vacation right now in an exotic location such as the Maldives or the Virgin Islands with his wife and kids. They are on the beach with drinks in their hands, enjoying the sounds of the seagulls as the ocean waves lull them to sleep. Their kids are happily throwing sand in the air and building sand castles without a care in the world. The owner's assistant is responding to the emails and dealing with a few small activities until the owner returns from the magical vacation we dream of.

We **ALL** deserve that vacation. That's right, we all deserve it. I also don't mean once before we die, I mean quarterly, or even more frequently. Why not? Seriously, why not? Here is why not. Most of us will never step out of our comfort zone to try something new. Something riskier with much higher rewards. We are content with that *job* I described earlier. We are satisfied with working the same dead-end job and complaining about the boss. You and your coworkers sit at the break table talking about how you hate coming here and how they don't pay you enough. You talk about how you can do a better job than the supervisor and that the only reason that the supervisor got that position is that he grew up with the owner's kid.

You deserve better. However, no one is going to give you a better life or better work conditions. You must decide to take action. There are opportunities out there. My wife and I have managed to create a better experience for our family and ourselves through REAL ESTATE. In this book, I am going to provide you the step by step process of getting started as a Real Estate Investor. We began investing in Clarksville, Tennessee. We have read so many books on property investing. Many of those books have helped us get to where we are today. However, there was never a book that gave us the step by step of starting our business. We had to learn many lessons the hard way and unfortunately, in real estate, the hard way is usually very costly. This book is designed to help you get started on the right foot and to avoid some of the beginner mistakes that most of us make without the guidance of a mentor.

THE FOUNDATION

Step 1-Why?

As cliché as it is, you must identify your "why." Why do you want to start your own business? Why do you want to quit your job? Maybe it's to spend more time with your family. Some people want to be millionaires, some want to buy the biggest home in the city, some want power and fame. My "why" is simple, I want to own my time. I want to be able to stay home with my wife and kids. I want to be ready to go on vacation whenever we decide to go, not when my boss says that I can take a vacation. I want to spend as much quality time on this earth as I possibly can. As I said before, we are not put here only to work. That is not the kind of life that I want to live.

I want to provide a better example for my kids. They deserve better than getting caught in the "40/40/40" trap. 40/40/40 eludes to the average person working <u>40 hours a week</u>, for <u>40 years</u>, hoping to make at least <u>40 dollars an hour</u> so that they can retire and live on less than what they were making for 40 years. As a society, we have accepted the 40/40/40 trap as the only option. We have seen our friends and family fall into the trap for generations and we accept it as, "that is just the way it is." That should not be the way it is. You deserve better and so does your family.

When you identify *why* you *need* to start your own business, it will be your motivating factor to push through. It's no secret that starting a business takes a lot of long days and hard work. However, if you do it right, those long days won't last as long as you may think. As you continue to pour your time and effort into building your business you will slowly notice that you have a little bit more free time. You have a little bit more money to enjoy with the family. There is a reason and a method to the madness.

When you are up late at night or encounter a minor setback, remember why you are doing this. Trust me; it's worth the extra stress, it's worth the late nights, it's worth the initial struggle. Keep the goal in mind. I'm doing all of this because...

Step 2-Education

Seven months! For seven months, every day after my day job, I came home and began plugging away. I bought into a fancy real estate education system that cost me almost **$30,000**. Yes, that isn't a typo, $30,000. I would get home around 6:00 p.m. and go straight to my computer and begin taking classes. I would finish a course and go to my documents that I had saved from the education company. I would spend hours and hours formatting and refining the materials to fit my business. On the weekends I would go out and put signs at intersections. You have seen them, "WE BUY HOUSES, CALL...". Yep, that was me.

Finally! I got my first house under contract. At this point, I have paid out so much money and I had received $0 in return. During those first few months I began to second-guess my decision. Doubt set in. I had spent so much money and had nothing to show for it. I had taken that money that could have been used for my family and spent it on a dream that had not produced anything.

Should you spend that kind of money on real estate coaching? Maybe, maybe not. There are many resources out there that are much less expensive. I buy audiobooks on Amazon for under $15 all the time. I listen to them in my vehicle or while I'm relaxing around the house. For your reading pleasure, I highly recommend *"Rich Dad Poor Dad"* by Robert Kiyosaki, the *"E-Myth Revisited"* by Michael Gerber, *"The 4 Hour Work Week"* by Timothy Ferriss, any book written by the "Bigger Pockets" guys, and many others that I'll reference later in this book.

Step 3-Research Your Market

Realize now that not all markets are created equal. Depending on where you are living/conducting business, you may not ever want to be a landlord because the laws aren't landlord friendly. You may wish only to flip homes because the profit margins are just too good to pass up. You may only want to deal with apartments for insurance purposes. Every market is different.

Speaking from experience, when I watched the DIY channel and saw the investors making well over $100,000 for flipping a house, I couldn't wait to start flipping. I learned very quickly those were not our numbers in my market of Clarksville, Tennessee. In my market, an average flip will net the investor between $18,000 and $30,000. Those are still significant numbers when done the right way. If I can utilize systems and leverage to flip a house, and only use about 8 hours of my time to do so, that is an excellent return for my efforts. If I net $18,000 for 8 hours of work, that equals $2,250 an hour on that project. I don't know of any jobs that offer that type of hourly compensation.

The point is that your real estate education can make or break you. You will never know everything about real estate. There are always new strategies, rules, laws, and regulations that will affect your business. The day that you stop learning is the beginning of the end for your business. The market is forever changing. Stay in touch with your market, stay in touch with local trends, and enjoy creating and building your legacy.

Chapter 2: Entity, Systems, and Accounts

Time to get creative... what is going to be the name of your business? How are you going to structure your business as in LLC, S-CORP, DBA, etc.? Depending on your strategy, a CPA will advise you one way or the other. We use an S-CORP and have had great success with it. Talk to a CPA before making that decision. Don't take to long trying to decide your business name. Pick a name and go with it. A wise man once told me, "You can have a perfect product or a completed product." Don't waste too much time.

 A CPA or an attorney will be able to help you establish your entity. Our CPA can send in all the documentation to both state and local authorities to receive our Employer Identification Number (EIN) and all the necessary business licenses. Having an expert perform these steps for you will ensure that they are done correctly and on time. Yes, you may save money by doing it yourself, but realize early on that your time is more valuable than your money. I have no problem paying a professional to do something better and more efficiently than I can.

Another piece of advice that I received early on is to build your business as if you are going to sell it later on down the road. I don't recommend using city names or family names unless they are very common. For example, I wouldn't be able to sell "Adam Johnson Home Buyers" to anyone. Start with the end goal in mind. Our goal is to sell our business after 15 years and retire early. Begin your business with an exit strategy. Your exit strategy may be to sell the company at a later date, to bring on partners at a later time, or even to hand the business down to your children or grandchildren.

Even though you have no business yet, start acquiring and learning systems. Systems will streamline your company and its processes. Systems will make your business more mechanical and alleviate a lot of the human error that we all have within us. More efficiency and fewer errors equal higher profit margins. Below are a few of the systems and accounts that I highly recommend setting up, learning, and utilizing in the early days of your business.

1. <u>Website</u> — In today's world you **MUST** have an internet presence. If you are not online you will always be playing catch up with other investors that are online. You can buy your domain from godaddy.com, Google G Suite, SquareSpace.com, etc. You can actually have multiple domains under one G Suite, which is the provider that we use. Nowadays, before a client calls you or decides to work with you, they will conduct a google search. If they can't find anything, because you have no internet presence, they are likely going to a competitor.

2. <u>Email Account</u> — I recommend tailoring your email to your domain name. You can go cheap and use something generic like <u>homebuyers@yahoo.com</u>. In the eyes of other professionals and clients, having and using an email with your domain looks more professional. We use the Google G Suite. You can always connect with me at <u>Adam@JoProInvestments.com</u> or <u>Adam@1stStepLLC.com</u>.

3. <u>CRM</u>— Customer Relations Management software (CRM). You'll need a system to track your interested clients, your contractors, other investors, bankers, realtors, cleaners, attorneys, buyers, etc. We currently use RealeFlow.com. RealeFlow hosts our website and serves as our CRM. Most CRMs have a way to mail-merge. A mail merge will allow you to send multiple emails to clients, but it will appear as if you only sent the email to one client. You can send thousands of personalized emails with one click.

4. <u>Phone Service</u> — Do not start with using your personal number. Your business is a separate entity. Treat it as such. We began by using 8x8.com. We have since switched to Grasshopper. Many of our clients also use Google Voice. If you are a landlord you never want to have a tenant texting you at 9:00 pm about anything. None of our tenants have our personal information. You also don't want to have your personal number all over social media or local billboards when you are advertising for new sellers.

5. <u>Accounting</u> — This is my least favorite part of the job; however, it is probably the most important. You

MUST track your incoming and outgoing cash down to the penny. It may not seem like much, until you have 18 rentals or you are flipping 12 homes a year. Come tax time; you will wish that you had tracked your expenses. I highly recommend using QuickBooks. QuickBooks is so easy that a caveman like me can use it.

6. <u>Social Media</u> — As I stated before, you must have an internet presence. To add to that thought you must be on social media. Create a business page on Facebook and Instagram at a minimum. Both of those accounts are free, and that is where most of your clients spend a decent amount of their time. You can look on Pinterest.com or download the app for ideas on when to post on what mediums. On Pinterest, you can search things like, "Social Media Marketing," "How to set up my business page on Facebook and Instagram," etc. A very high percentage of our leads come from Facebook.

7. <u>Signing Software</u> — Throughout your business, you will have to send and sign many documents. Purchase Agreements, Lease Agreements, Change Orders, etc., are going to have to be signed. We use DocuSign.com to fit this need. Instead of emailing a

document to a client, having them print it out, sign it, scan it back in, and send it back to us, we use DocuSign. DocuSign allows clients, contractors, realtors, and everyone in between to digitally sign all documents. All parties have the same date and time stamp as to when the signatures were made. This is beneficial in the event there is a disagreement over when something was sent or signed. It doesn't happen often, but it does happen.

8. Cloud — A cloud is necessary for keeping your files always at reach. We use Microsoft OneDrive as our cloud server. A big mistake that new investors make is saving docs on their desktop or personal computer. That does them no good when they are meeting with a banker and the banker says they need X, Y, and Z. At any given moment, from my phone or anywhere else in the world, I can access all the business documents that I have ever uploaded. Also, once you have an assistant, you can give them access to the entire cloud, or a specific folder that applies to their part of the business. You always need your information readily available.

9. Rental Software — If you are beginning your real estate business with the intentions of landlording, I

highly recommend software to streamline the process. We have been using Buildium.com for the past four years, and we have had a great experience. Buildium is an all-encompassing software that allows you to run credit and background checks on potential tenants, enables you to receive payments online from tenants, and manages and stores documents like rental agreements and tenant identification, amongst others. The software sends out auto-reminders to tenants and keeps records of repairs that have been requested and completed on each property. It also allows the tenants to pay online so there is no need to drive to the bank or send a check. We, along with our tenants, love how user-friendly the program is.

10. <u>Bank Accounts</u> — Immediately set up checking, savings, and credit card accounts for your new business. Whether you are buying to flip or to hold, you'll need these accounts set up. Currently, we use our business checking account for cash flow purposes. We use the business savings account for the rental deposits. Also, we use the business credit card for most purchases throughout the month to accrue rewards. We typically

pay off our credit card balances each month. I highly recommend applying for a Line of Credit (LOC). A line of credit can be used for that opportunity that you didn't see coming. Occasionally, I'll get a call from a realtor about a house that needs $20,000 of rehab. Instead of using my money, I'll borrow from my LOC, rehab the property, and then pay off my LOC once the property is sold. So essentially, I am acquiring and repairing a home without my money. I use bank money.

By setting up these systems and accounts, you'll make your life much simpler. Your business will run much more efficiently and you won't feel so much like an employee of your own company. As you grow and find a niche, you may find other systems to employ. Continue to adapt your business to be more effective, efficient, and profitable.

Chapter 3: Build Your Team

Contrary to popular belief, you cannot run your business by yourself. You will need help. No matter how smart you are, how determined you are, or how great you think you are, you can't be the best at everything. Yes, you are the CEO/President of your company. Yes, you have the final authorization for everything that happens within your company. However, you need to build a team of advisors and other professionals to assist you along the way.

Face Time

Google "Real Estate Investor Association" (REIA) in your area. Most medium and large cities have these groups. They typically meet once a week or at least once a month. The meetings are open to anyone interested in real estate. They are usually free and you can start building your team while you are there. I'll cover more about "your team" later in the chapter. At these meetings you will meet realtors, other investors, wholesalers, private money lenders, hard money lenders, carpenters, plumbers, stagers, electricians, etc. The meetings usually have a theme for each session. They may focus on ways to acquire new rentals, what market is best for wholesalers, or how to structure your business for asset protection and many others.

Drive around your town and look for other "We Buy Houses" signs. Call those numbers. Introduce yourself and see if they will agree to meet with you. Be upfront and tell them that you are a new investor in the area and that you'd like to meet and ask a few questions. Usually, investors won't turn down a free meal. I called the first number on a similar sign and to this day that first call has been paramount to our success.

Ask those investors for recommendations. Which banks do they use, who is a good handyman, who is a good CPA that understands real estate? Plan and have your questions either in your head or in front of you. I recommend not having a pen and paper out, personally. Build a rapport and ask a few questions. Be personable and sell yourself. Then schedule another meeting more formal with your note-taking materials handy.

Key Personnel

CPA

First and foremost, find a Great CPA. Not just any CPA will do. Real estate is an entirely different business than most. There are many other tax benefits and write-offs that many other industries may or may not receive. You **MUST** have a CPA that understands Real Estate. Talk to other investors in the area and ask them who they recommend. If you start to hear the same name a few times, BINGO, that also needs to be your CPA.

That being said, you get what you pay for, and that goes for any part of real estate. The CPA that the pros are using probably won't be the cheapest. However, everything in real estate is about the long game. I don't mind paying my CPA precisely what he or she is worth when they save me tens of thousands of dollars a year. Don't be cheap and get your friend to do your taxes. Get a professional.

Real Estate Attorney

As before, not just any attorney will do. Don't get the cheapest or a "guy" that your friend knows. Interview a few attorneys to ensure that they understand your methods of acquiring homes. Whether or not you are buying traditionally, with investor money, owner finance, rent to own, or any other fashion, the attorney must understand your business. An attorney will also provide advice and look over all your legal documents. They'll probably have purchase agreements, lease agreements, etc. that will apply to your business in the city and state of which you are operating.

Title Company

Not all title companies are the same. Also, not all laws are the same from state to state. Walk into any title company and sit down with the first person that makes eye contact with you. Once again, explain to them what you are doing and what you hope to accomplish. Ask them about their guidelines and timelines. How quickly they can close your transactions is very important. Show them your purchase agreement to get their input and to make sure that it abides by the state and local laws. If you don't have a contract, ask them for one.

Contractors

You can find contractors in many ways. Start by asking other investors and search on Facebook and Craigslist. The most important thing with contractors is the interview process. I can write a few pages on lessons learned from dealing with contractors; however, in an effort to keep this book short and to the point, we'll hit the key points.

1. Receive proof that they are licensed. Ensure the contractors carry at least $1,000,000 in insurance.

2. Before a contractor ever begins the first project, have them fill out a W-9 Form. This will not only save you at the end of the year, but it also confirms the legitimacy of the contractor. If a contractor is not comfortable signing the standard W-9, send them on their way.

3. Almost all contractors say the can do everything. Well, they can't. Not one person has mastered every aspect of drywall, plumbing, electrical, countertops, etc. Each of them will have a few areas that they aren't quite

good at, so ask them, "What type of work are you not great at doing? What type of work do you typically sub out?"

4. Documentation is everything. I give my contractors a "Scope of Work" for each project that spells out precisely what is to be completed. Before the contractor begins, he gives me his total project cost, in writing, so there are no surprises. We sign and date everything.

5. Never pay up front. **ONLY PAY FOR COMPLETED WORK**. Part of my documentation is the payment schedule. For example, I may pay $2,000 once the demo is completed. Then once the drywall work is completed another check will be cut. NEVER pay for something that has not been completed.

6. Always keep your word. If you agree to pay X on this date, then that is what you do. Once you find a good contractor, keep them happy. They'll make you tons of money in the upcoming years.

Electricians and Plumbers

I highly recommend having a licensed electrician and plumber separate from your contractor for a few reasons. Those certifications and licenses are very specific and most general contractors won't have them. Also, if you hire a general contractor to take care of plumbing or electrical, many times they are going to hire a licensed plumber or electrician and then add 10-20 percent of their fee to what they are charging you. Example, the electrician charges the contractor $500 for new wiring, then the contractor charges you $600 for that service.

Painters

Hire a painter that has a paint crew. For the first few years we had a painter that was a one-man team. It would take him a week to paint a house. He was always booked so we had to let him know weeks in advance. That is not always possible. We hired a painter that had a four-man crew and we were blown away at how fast and less expensive that he operated. Because our current painter has a team, he has much more flexibility and is usually able to get to our new homes with five days' notice.

Realtors

There are many "investor friendly" realtors out there. Realtors are valuable for many reasons. They have access to the MLS. They get phone calls all the time for homes that are not sellable or need repairs and the owners can't afford those repairs. They get phone calls from buyers with bad credit. They see homes all day long and can, for a referral fee, send you leads that don't fit their criteria.

Cleaning Crew

Renting or selling, the homes must be cleaned. I recommend hiring professionals. They are experienced and know what to look for. Plus, some houses take 4-5 hours of cleaning and scrubbing to get ready. That time can be spent by you, the investor, on your business instead of cleaning.

Photographer

We have bought many homes that were listed for months with a realtor with little or no interest. I discovered that when I pulled up the listing on Zillow, the pictures were taken with an iPhone. From my experience, you can probably connect the quality of the photos with the lack of interest and showings for the property.

Find a good photographer. Ask realtors in your area for the contact information of their photographers. There is a big difference between family photography and real estate photography. We pay our photographer $100 per home and an additional $50 for a professional quality video walk-thru of the home. That $150 is more than worth it. Simply put, a good photographer can get you great tenants or qualified buyers in a very short time.

Understand that you are one person. You can't possibly do everything all the time. I learned early on to hire help. Leverage other people's talent and time. If you can pay someone to do a small task that will free up your time, do it! You are much more important and valuable to the business being out there making contacts, signing contracts, and making deals. The goal is to build a team and pay people so that you ONLY do what ONLY you can do.

Chapter 4: Documents

Put it in writing. Start a good habit from day one by documenting everything. There is a lot more to being an investor than a simple contract to buy a home. Unfortunately, there are many people out there that may be looking for a loophole or a way to get one over on the investor. From the first call with a potential buyer, start documenting. Before the contractor walks through the home for the first time, document. Before you show a prospective tenant a new rental, have specific documentation required for them to see the house. Below is, in no particular order, just a few of the documents that we use every day.

- *Offer to Contract and Purchase Agreement*—This is the contract between your business and the home sellers. There a few mandatory things that go into a contract to make it legally binding. Each state may have different guidelines so make sure that you consult an attorney to ensure that the contract that you are using is legally binding. Essential parts of the contract include, but are not limited to:

- Purchase price
- Closing date
- Legal names of buyer and seller
- Closing costs
- Tax information
- Closing location
- Contingencies

• *Scope of Work (SOW)*—The SOW outlines precisely what you want the contractor to repair. Never tell a contractor to fix anything that you didn't previously agree to in writing before the work is completed. Our method is to stick to the SOW unless there is a Change Order or another form of record like text or email. Before the first board is demolished, the contractor provides an estimate, in writing, for record purposes. I have seen too many times where new investors didn't have a clear scope of work and just walked through a property with a contractor pointing out what needed to be done. Then, once the project was complete, the contractor billed the investor thousands more than what was initially or verbally agreed to.

- *Independent Contractor Agreement*—This is an agreement between the investor and the contractor that outlines not only the total price of the project but also the completion date. Early on I had a few projects that ran a lot longer than we had verbally agreed upon. Now, we sign a contract that outlines the completion date. For every day that the contractor goes over that date, the contractor pays us $250.
- *Rental/Lease Agreement*—This is probably the second most crucial document to our business, the first being the Purchase Agreement. The rental agreement outlines many important details listed below, but are not limited to:
  - Who can occupy the home
  - How much will they pay monthly
  - Late fees for late payments
  - Beginning and end of the lease term
  - Rules of the property
    - No smoking
    - No parking on the lawn

- No loud music
- Etc.
  - Inspection notices
  - Pet fees
  - When payments are due
- *Addendums*—Many times after a purchase agreement is signed, or even a lease agreement, you and the other party may agree to change terms. A few examples are:
  - Change of the closing date
  - Change of the purchase price due to an issue discovered during the inspection
  - Modification of the lease agreement due to an additional pet being part of the household
- *Power of Attorney*—There are many creative ways to work in real estate. Many times, you'll have to act fast which may require a POA to be present for yourself or another party to sign to execute a transaction.
- *Deeds*—The deed shows ownership of each property. Many buyers and sellers do not understand the difference between a deed and a mortgage. Many think they are the same. To simplify the terms, the deed

shows ownership and mortgage shows who is financially responsible for the property. Your closing attorney or title company will ensure that the deeds have all the correct information and is not "clouded" with negative information.

There are many more documents required to run a successful real estate business and to protect the company while doing so. Your real estate attorney is an excellent place to start when you begin compiling your documents. Purchase them from your attorney and then put your heading on them and put your logo as the watermark. Don't be frugal when it comes to paying for documents. Remember, someone took the time to do the research and to put those documents together. Pay them for their time and expertise.

Chapter 5: Strategies

Let me start by saying that there are MANY strategies when it comes to real estate. I'll talk about the five most common that I see every day. I'll cover the pros and cons of each along with my personal experience.

Wholesaling

Wholesaling is just what you think it is. Think about a store that sells clothing. Walmart will buy clothes at wholesale price, and then upcharge the consumer in order to make a profit. To do this, Walmart must first find the clothing supplier, negotiate a reasonable price that provides their desired profit margin, and then bring that product into the store to sell it to the consumer to achieve that desired profit.

In real estate, some people do almost the exact same thing. Instead of negotiating a fair purchase price on a pair of socks, a wholesaler will negotiate the sales price and terms of a house. They will get the house under contract at a wholesale price and then find a consumer, or another investor, to purchase the home for a finder's fee or an "assignment fee."

I am going to use a wholesale deal I executed as an example. Here is the quick rundown. I received a call from a seller who had a home that needed a lot of work. I went to view the home and to get an estimate of how much it would cost to repair the home. The home was already paid off by the longtime owner, but the owner didn't have the funds to make the repairs. The owner needed to sell the home quickly in order to move out of the area.

I sent the address to my realtor to get an idea of what the home would be worth at top dollar once all repairs were made. The home was worth about $140,000 After Repair Value (ARV) and it needed about $28,000 in repairs. I negotiated with the seller to sell her home for $65,000. I got the home under contract for $65,000. I then went and found a buyer and I sold, or assigned, the buyer my interest in the home. I sold my interest for $6,000. So, the buyer bought the contract that I had negotiated and a $6,000 assignment fee for a total investment of $71,000.

So, let us recap the deal above. The seller received $65,000 for a home that was unsellable. A buyer got a $71,000 home that needed about $28,000 in repairs. The total investment was $99,000 for a house that would be worth $140,000. I received $6,000 for negotiating the entire deal. Total time invested in this deal was about 6 hours. In this deal I made $1,000 an hour. Not too bad. The seller was able to sell her home, the rehab investor was able to buy a home under market value to be able to make a profit once it was sold, and I received a fee for bringing the two together. It was indeed a win-win-win situation.

Buy, Rehab, Sell

If you have ever seen an episode on HGTV or any of the others like that, this is the strategy that you are probably most aware of. The TV shows are about 20% reality. There is so much more to the process than they show you. They make it sound too easy. They'll say they bought a house for $150,000, rehabbed the home for $50,000, and sold the home for $300,000 which is a profit of $100,000. **NO, THEY DIDN'T**. The TV shows rarely talk about the closing costs, the holding costs, busting their timelines, going over budget, the flooring company being out of stock of the tile that you always use, and the list goes on and on.

Flipping homes breaks down to simple math. Everyone has their formula to see if it is a good deal. I'll simplify the process for you. Here is a typical breakdown of how I use backward math to see if the home is a good deal or if I should move onto the next one. I start with what the home will sell for after I have made all the repairs (**ARV-After Repair Value**). I include holding costs and closing costs, my rehab budget, and my minimum desired profit once the deal is completed. This will give me my Maximum Allowable Offer (MAO) to the seller for their home.

$200,000 – ARV

-$20,000 – Closing Costs (to sell the home with a realtor and pay the closing cost for the seller)

-$25,000 – Rehab

-$5,000 – Holding Costs (mortgage, utilities, insurance, misc.)

-$5,000 – Financing Cost (cost for me to borrow money from a bank or private money lender)

-$25,000 – Desired profit

$120,000 - Maximum Allowable Offer

The numbers above are merely round numbers to show you a simple way to calculate offers. Some investors have super complicated algorithms that blow my mind. I keep things simple and we've had success using this formula.

The last thing I'll say about flipping homes, I highly recommend getting a home inspection before you buy any home. With my sellers, we come to a purchase price agreement. Once we are under contract I get a home inspection to make sure that I'm not getting into much bigger problems. I tell my sellers that I only care about the "Big 5" which are HVAC, Plumbing, Electrical, Foundation, and the Roof. If any of those systems have significant issues, I have the ability to renegotiate or walk away from a bigger problem.

"BRRRR"

Buy, Rehab, Rent, Refinance, Repeat! This the most preferred strategy to build long term wealth. Buy the home, rehab the home, find a renter to pay for your financing of the home, refinance (refi) the home to pull the cash out of the home that you put into the home, then do it again.

Here is how the numbers work using the example I gave earlier in the chapter. We buy a home for $120,000. I use bank financing that will provide me with 80% of the purchase price ($96,000) and 100% of the rehab cost ($25,000). That means that I must bring $24,000 to closing. So, I or my business, will have $24,000 into a home that will be worth $200,000. After we complete the process of buying, rehabbing, and renting the home, it's time for me to go back to the bank to "cash-out refi." This means that I will refinance the home to pull the equity out to use on another investment.

The bank will usually give you up to 80% of the ARV when you refinance. On a $200,000 home, we could get up to $160,000. From the $160,000 we pay off the bank for the original mortgage ($96,000) and the rehab cost ($25,000) which totals $121,000 leaving us with $39,000. So, not only have we made back our initial investment of $24,000, remember that is what we had to pay at closing for purchasing the home, but we have also created a net profit of $15,000.

This is called infinite returns. You have none of your money in the investment. You have an asset with a renter that is paying your mortgage, and you've pulled out all the money that you ever put into the home. You have used bank money to acquire an asset with infinite returns. That is a beautiful thing.

Now, what do you do with the $39,000? You buy two more houses using the same strategy. You can use this strategy and multiply your money every few months.

Lease Option (Rent to Own)

How can you assist a seller that may not have enough equity to sell their home and cover the closing costs? One way is by utilizing a lease option. Notice the word "Option." This means that you can rent a home with the "option" to purchase. This is commonly referred to as "rent to own."

Scenario-Steve and Stacy bought their home nine months ago. Three weeks ago, Steve received notification that his job is promoting him to a general management position that is out of state. Steve and Stacy have not owned the home long enough for the home to appreciate enough to cover the estimated 10% in closing costs when traditionally selling a home. Steve and Stacy have only heard the horror stories about local property management companies and aren't sure what they are going to do with their home.

Mr. Investor sits down with Steve and Stacy and runs through the Lease Option proposal. Mr. Investors offers to buy Steve and Stacy's home for the full market value in today's market. The home is currently worth $150,000. Steve and Stacy now owe $146,000. Mr. Investor negotiates that he will pay Steve and Stacy $150,000 within the next five years. Until he can purchase the home, the Mr. Investor will pay Steve and Stacy $1,200 a month in rent.

Now that Mr. Investor has the home under contract to purchase for $150,000 in no more than five years, and he has negotiated the monthly rental amount, Mr. Investor can then go and find a buyer to "Lease Option" from him. However, the terms will be much different. Mr. Investor takes into account the market appreciation rate in the area and estimates that the home will be worth $195,000 in the next five years. Mr. Investor finds a tenant-buyer that needs a little time to clear up some personal credit issues and would love to buy the house in a few years for the asking price of $195,000.

The lease option buyer sees the price more than favorable considering the average market appreciation in the area. The lease option buyer and Mr. Investor negotiate that the buyer will rent from Mr. Investor for $1,500 a month for no more than five years. That will give Mr. Investor a positive cash flow of $300 a month. If the term goes for the entire five years, Mr. Investor will profit $18,000 in passive rental income, not to mention the profit that Mr. Investor will receive when the home is sold.

The above example is considered a "sandwich lease option", where the investor was in the middle negotiating terms between the seller and the end buyer. The investor provided the seller with a solution and then found an end buyer and provided them with an opportunity as well.

We have created a win-win-win situation. The sellers were able to hand over responsibility to an investor. The investor will be paying the sellers rent until the investor can bring $150,000 to buy the home. The tenant-buyer can get into a home that will soon be theirs and at a fair rate.

The tenant buyer will buy the home from the investor for $195,000. The investor will take that money and then pay the seller $150,000. The investor has made a $45,000 gross profit minus closing costs, if any, and other miscellaneous expenses as part of the real estate transaction. On top of the profit received when the buyer purchased the home, the investor also received monthly cash flow in the form of rent for the property.

Subject-To

"Subject-To" is one of the lesser known strategies in the world of real estate investing. This means that an investor will purchase a home "subject-to" the seller's financing staying in place. The deed, or ownership transfers, but the mortgage remains in the seller's name.

Why would any seller do this? Here are just a few reasons. The seller may be behind on payments and can't afford to make the necessary repairs to sell the home. The seller has no equity. The seller has had a bad run of tenants. The list goes on and on. We have dealt with many situations and we are proud to have the knowledge and creativity to help homeowners in these circumstances.

This technique of "Subject-To" is our primary means of acquiring new homes. We have purchased homes from individuals that had emergencies come up just months after they had bought their homes. Of course, the home had not gone up in value enough for the seller to cover all of the closing costs associated with a traditional real estate transaction using realtors and title companies. By us having the knowledge and systems in place, we were able to offer these sellers a way to get out from under the responsibility of paying on a vacant house or dealing with tenants.

We have purchased homes that were behind on mortgage payments and even homes that would not qualify for a loan due to the home needing repairs. We have purchased homes that had negative equity or homes that the homeowners couldn't afford due to a personal situation. Subject-To is a unique and powerful way to help families and acquire new properties.

Wendy Patton wrote a very informative book regarding the last two strategies called, *"Investing in Real Estate with Lease Options and "Subject-To" Deals."* The book goes into great detail on both of these "low and no-money-down" techniques. There are many books on the subject and everyone structures their deals differently.

Once again, there are many other strategies. Within the five that we talked about in this chapter there are many more details and things to keep in mind. There are many books on each strategy. This book is designed to get you started and to take action. Once you start, you'll develop your niche. I recommend being absolutely great at one thing instead of trying to dabble in everything.

Chapter 6: The Process of the Purchase

So, you have started marketing and your phone rings. What do you do? Here is a typical rundown of the steps that you'll need to systemize in your business to make the process as efficient as possible.

Step 1-The phone rings. Here it is, you have your first potential property. How you handle the initial call is critical to the way this entire deal is going to happen. If you do not appear confident, the seller may not trust in your ability to help them. If you are too pushy, you may scare away the seller. If you talk too much, you may annoy the seller. So, what do you do? Simple, you introduce yourself. "Hi, this is Steve with insert company, how can I help you?" Let the person on the phone talk. Within the first few seconds, you'll figure out a lot. Listen to not only their words but the tone in their voice. I always ask them, "So what's the situation?

Why are you looking to sell your home?" Again, listen to their words and the tone in their voice.

You can typically determine how motivated they are to sell their home within the first minute of the conversation. If they call and say that they are "shopping around," they are not worth your time. You are looking to work with the motivated sellers. A few reasons that a seller may be motivated to sell could be that they are moving out of the area, getting divorced, tired of dealing with tenants, bad management company, need to downsize, need to upsize, behind on payments, etc.

I have received phone calls from sellers that try to tell me what they will and will not do. If a seller ever calls and tries to tell you what to do, they don't need you. Politely refer them to a realtor and don't waste another minute. You are a unique home buyer. You only deal with sellers that "need" your services. If a seller can sell their home on the open market for full price and cover all closing costs, they probably don't need you. However, if a seller is in one of the situations that I mentioned earlier, they need your services and you should do everything in your power to create a win-win situation to help them and yourself.

Step 2-Seller Questionnaire. Depending on which book you read or which mentor you work with, many advisors will tell you to run the caller through a Seller Questionnaire while you have them on the phone. This is done to pre-qualify a seller or to determine if the lead is a hot lead or a dead lead.

I do this step a little differently. While on the phone with the sellers I ask them for their email address. I tell them, "It's been great talking to you, Mr. Seller. Can you please provide me with your email address? I'll send you a quick little seller questionnaire for you to fill out. I do this to build the profile for your property in my system and to get basic information about the property. This will help us build the profile for your home and better assist you moving forward."

Why would I do it that way? Mainly because sellers may feel pressured or defensive about you directly asking specific questions about their home. I send them an email with the *Typeform* link to my Seller Questionnaire. This allows them to answer pertinent questions in the comfort of their own home. I ask them to complete it within 24 hours. Also, I've just put the power in their hands to show me exactly how motivated they are. I've had clients fill out the questionnaire in four minutes. I immediately put them at the top of my list and we bought their house in 12 days. I've had other clients take three days, fill out half of the questions, and the deal never gets close to closing.

Step 3-Comp the Property. Run comparables or "comps" on the subject property. I typically ask a realtor to do this for me. The realtor will take the subject property and look for "like" homes that have sold in the area of the subject home. For example, your subject property is a home with three beds, two baths, no garage, with 1,100 square feet of living space. The realtor will set up similar parameters in their system to view "like" properties that have recently sold. They typically will get at least three similar properties and take the average sales, per square foot. Example: House #1 is a three bedroom, two baths, 1,320 square feet that sold for $150,000. If you divide the sales price of $150,000 by the square footage of 1,320, you'll see that the home was sold for $113.64 a square foot. The realtor will do the same for at least two more similar properties to get the average price per square foot.

I always ask my realtors to give me the top dollar amount of the subject property. This is the amount that I can sell the home for once all repairs have been completed (ARV). I use this number as the foundation for the rest of the process. For example, if the home has an "ARV" of $200,000, but the home also needs $40,000 of repairs, I know where to begin my negotiations with the sellers. I also know what my Maximum Allowable Offer (MAO) is as well. The MAO is the amount of money that I will not go above on this particular home during the negotiation of the home.

Step 4-The Viewing. You have received the Seller Questionnaire and have determined that the information meets your criteria to move forward. You can either call the sellers or as I like to do, email them to schedule the viewing. I like to email because it serves as a record with a date/time stamp.

The viewing of the property is the most essential step of the entire process. Here is where you first get to meet the seller and to see the condition of the property. When meeting for the first time, don't go right into business. Always take the first few minutes to build rapport. You can talk about anything as long as you get the seller to speak. The seller needs to see you as a person instead of a businessman/businesswoman.

After rapport has been built, it's time for the walkthrough. One technique is for the investor to walk through the home with a pen and paper writing down all deficiencies. This is done to ensure that the investor doesn't miss small things so that the investor may more accurately calculate repair costs, if any. However, this can put the homeowner on the defensive. Many homeowners may find it insulting to walk through their homes pointing out everything that is "wrong" with the home. They may also feel that the investor is just trying to make more money off of them.

I prefer a subtler technique. I walk through making mental notes of everything I see. After you've been through a few hundred homes, you develop a standardized way to view homes. I know what I'm looking for and I have a great idea of what materials and labor cost will be to fix many items in homes. I do my walkthrough with the sellers. I ask the seller what needs to be repaired or updated. Many times, the sellers will lead me to the problem areas. I do this to involve the seller. In this technique, the seller and I both see and agree that item "x" needs to be repaired. So, when I bring up item "x" during the negotiations, the seller is less likely to be on the defensive.

Step 5-Analyzing the deal. We've met with the seller and we've viewed the home. We have an idea of the cost to get the home ready for new tenants or ready for the market to be sold at top dollar. Now we put all the numbers on paper. Below is an example of the breakdown from a previous chapter in this book.

$200,000 – ARV

-$20,000 – Closing Costs (to sell the home with a realtor and pay the closing cost for the seller)

-$25,000 – Rehab

-$5,000 – Holding Costs (mortgage, utilities, misc.)

-$5,000 – Financing Cost (cost for me to borrow money from a bank or private money lender)

-$25,000 – Desired profit

$120,000 - Maximum Allowable Offer

Is my first offer on the home $120,000? Absolutely not! Always give yourself room to negotiate. I would probably begin negotiations on this home at $105,000. Of course, the seller isn't going to accept my initial offer, as you should never do in negations. However, if during the negotiations I give in just a little bit and raise the amount to $120,000, the seller sees it as a little "give and take." The seller got a little more for their home, and I got a great asset that can potentially make us money down the road. Each deal must be a win-win.

Step 6-Contract and Due Diligence. Once we agree to terms, it is time to lock in the deal by getting the home under contract. This is the most critical document in the process. The contract is going to spell out the terms of the entire deal. This includes, but is not limited to: purchase price, purchase date, inspection clause, the condition of the property, type of deed, who the deed will be conveyed to, special conditions, taxes, the location of closing, etc.

I have a simple two-page contract that is mostly in layman terms. Know your contract! Be able to answer any questions from sellers regarding any of the terms and conditions within the contract. If the sellers are local, meet with the sellers to sign the contract. Early on in my career I would send the contract to the sellers via email and the sellers would not understand something within the contract. Give the contract to the sellers in person. Talk through the contract and build the trust between the sellers and yourself. At the end of the conversation, or sales presentation, "ASK FOR THE SALE." Zig Ziglar is big on, "always asking for the sale." Too many times a professional will give a presentation but never ask for the commitment of a signature from the sellers. Don't leave the house without asking for the sellers to sign the Purchase Agreement.

If the sellers are not local, no problem. I have met with many sellers via Google Meeting. Google Meeting is similar to Skype but I am able to share documents on their screen to be able to talk through the process. If the sellers aren't local, I use DocuSign to send my contracts to the sellers. I give the sellers 48 hours to view and sign the contract. That gives them time to take the contract to an attorney, seek counsel from friends and family, or to think it over. Keep in mind; time is of the essence. Give them a firm deadline and expiration date of your offer. If sellers see the contract offer as open-ended, they tend to take their time and not take your offer seriously. "My offer expires on Tuesday at 5:00 P.M. Let me know if you have any questions."

In the meantime, I'm ordering the home inspection, HVAC inspection, and the termite inspection. Sellers will ask me, "if you are buying my house as-is, why do you need an inspection." I say, "I am going to know exactly what I'm buying." Even though we did a walkthrough, I am not a trained home inspector. I'm an investor. I hire people who are better at certain jobs than I am to give me professional feedback. Very few times have I backed out of a deal based on the home inspection. If anything, the seller and I have been able to renegotiate terms due to a major end item, i.e., HVAC unit or roof not being serviceable. Always, always, always get an inspection. An inspection costs me about $300 but it has saved me from making much more costly mistakes. I once had a house under contract and the home inspection came back with multiple issues with the foundation. I then had a foundation specialist give me an assessment and an estimate of repairs. The estimate came back at about $4,000. I wasn't going to lose that much money on day one and the seller didn't want to pay for the repairs for his house. The $300 home inspection saved me a $4,000 foundation repair. We didn't purchase that home.

The home inspectors typically look at the HVAC system as part of their home inspection. However, that isn't their specialty. I recommend having a licensed HVAC tech to provide a full system diagnostic test to ensure that all components are working to maximum efficiency. My HVAC tech charges me $65 to conduct the diagnostic test, which is a small price to pay when the alternative could be replacing a $5,000 unit at my cost after the purchase has been completed.

Termite inspections are just as significant as the other inspections. If anything, we see more termite claims than major end items when acquiring a new property. As with anything, if there are termite issues, I will typically renegotiate with the seller to get the remediation paid for.

Step 7-Prepare for Closing. Once you are comfortable with the inspections and the terms of the agreement, it's time to prepare for closing. A typical closing takes place at a Title Company. This is simple and easy. You will send the title company the contract and they'll do the rest. The title company will conduct the "title search." This is a critical step. A title search is performed to ensure there are no liens against the property and that no one else has any claim to the property. Generally, in newer homes, this isn't an issue. However, when you buy a home that was built in 1968 and it has had 13 owners, you may see unusual activity. A title search is worth the extra money.

Once the title company has conducted the title search and has verified the mortgage payoff and banking information, you are cleared to close. You call the sellers and confirm the closing date/time/location.

Because I buy many homes from military members, my sellers are not always local. My attorney prepares the closing docs and emails the docs to the sellers. The sellers will then print the closing docs, get them notarized, and then FedEx the originals back to my attorney. At that point, my attorney calls and I go to the attorney's office to sign my portion of the closing docs. Once the closing docs are signed and notarized by both the sellers and buyers, the closing docs go to the county register of deeds office. The deed is recorded and now I officially have another property.

I use a personal attorney for my closings because we have developed that trust and working relationship. A title company is just as capable of closing on homes when the sellers are not local. Contact a local title company to ask them about their processes.

When you begin purchasing homes, you'll develop your way of doing things. Make checklists and flowcharts. Standardize your process as I have above. Do what works efficiently for you and standardize it so that you can hire on help to delegate some of those tasks. As I said before, build your business almost like a franchise. Make it so that you can hire on help and essentially have the company running smoothly without you being needed for day to day operations.

Chapter 7: Post Acquisition

Congratulations! You have purchased your first investment property! Now it is time to make your money work for you. As stated before, there are many strategies that we can discuss. I'm going to cover the two most common strategies which are 1) rehabbing to sell (flip) and 2) rehabbing to rent.

Rehab to Sell

You have just bought your subject property with the intention to rehab it and get it sold fast so that you can use the capital to buy more homes. Understand, the amount of money that you put into a rehab project will be relative to the location and the market. If you have purchased a three-bedroom starter home that is on the lower end of the spectrum, as far as price per square feet, you aren't going to go overboard with the repairs.

You make the home pleasant and neutral with minor upgrades that are with the modern trends.

Major repairs! To sell the home, you must repair EVERYTHING! Reason being, when the new buyer has their home inspector go through the home, you don't want a laundry list of repairs. Even though the repairs may be easy to rectify, some buyers can be easily scared away by a long list of deficiencies. Before I buy the home, I have a home inspection. I keep that report and when I give my scope of work to my contractor, I also hand him the home inspection that I received before I purchased the home. I tell the contractor to fix everything on the inspection. Be proactive, don't wait until you "have" to fix something. Take care of it up front.

Don't customize the home to your likings. You need to appeal to the masses by making the home neutral. Remember, you will never live in the home so don't design it for you and your family. As seemingly small a detail as it is, paint colors can and will deter many buyers. I recommend a neutral gray. We typically use "repose gray" which is not too light or dark and it goes with just about any décor. Flooring is very important. Ensure that the carpet, laminate, or hardwood flooring looks new and is in excellent condition. Many of the older homes we purchased had great original hardwood flooring that we merely refinished. Ensure that all of your hardware, i.e., door knobs and hinges, fixtures, faucets, etc., all match. You don't want some gold hinges, silver faucets, and oil bronze ceiling fans. If you are unsure of local market trends, talk with realtors in the area to get recommendations of finishes and level of upgrades that a particular area requires to be competitive in that market.

Now, if you are flipping a five bedroom home that is top of the line in the area in which you are operating, then this is a different story. Again, talk to a realtor or another investor in the area to get their recommendations on the types of finishes that should be put into a more beautiful home in the area. You don't want to "under" rehab your property. The name of the game is to make the home sellable at the price you desire to receive for the property without busting your budget.

Rehab to Rent

Preparing the home for rent isn't much different than it is to prepare the home for sale. However, you analyze materials and cost much differently. In rehabbing to rent, you are more of a bargain shopper. The home doesn't need the newest finishes and the greatest appliances. The home needs to be clean and presentable. You don't have to replace the roof immediately, or the HVAC system. You can let the property provide you with passive income for a few years and use that cash to make those types of repairs. As long as those repairs are in your budget when you run your numbers, let the property pay for itself.

Once the home is ready for new tenants, what do you do? The easy answer is to turn the property over to a management company. There are pros and cons of doing so. First a few of the advantages: 1) Takes the liability off you, the homeowner. 2) The management company must deal with tenants to include new tenant acquisitions. 3) The management company also deals with and schedules maintenance calls and repairs. 4) The management company typically has an attorney in the event a tenant must be evicted or sued for damages to the property. There are many more, but those are the few that we'll discuss in this section.

Now, for the cons with handing your rental property over to a management company: 1) The management company has nothing to lose. If the property sits vacant for weeks or even months, they aren't the ones having to pay the mortgage for said property. 2) Usually, management companies charge 10% of the gross rent. Keep that in mind when you do your calculations to determine your profit margins. If your mortgage is $700 and the rent for the said property is $1,000, the management company keeps 10% or $100 leaving you with a net profit of $200. Many management companies have other fees as well on top of the 10%. For example, they may charge a "new acquisitions" fee for getting that tenant. They may charge a fee for them to go to the property to conduct an inspection. Be sure to ask these questions and read the agreement thoroughly if you decide to list with a management company.

There are several books and programs discussing in great detail the mechanics behind both rehabbing to sell and preparing a home for rent. I like to listen to and read the teaching of *Bigger Pockets*. Brandon, one of the hosts on *Bigger Pockets*, believes in building wealth through rental real estate. I also subscribe to the practice of creating long term wealth by acquiring rental real estate.

Before you ever purchase a property, you should have a primary and alternate exit strategy for the property. Don't buy a property and then figure out what you are going to do. More often than not, an investor may purchase a home with the intent to flip and sell. For whatever reason, the home doesn't sell. A good alternative may be to rent the house for a year, let the market appreciate, have some cash flow, and then attempt to sell the home again.

Chapter 8: Service/Product

I believe Zig Ziglar said, "If you want to be rich, find a way to make many people happy." What he meant was to provide a service or a product and bring joy to many people. Depending on how you look at real estate, it can be a service or a product. The service is how you are assisting people and being creative with your solutions to people's real estate needs or situations. To help people buy, sell, or rent a home is a powerful opportunity and will have a positive effect or impact on a family's life. The product can be land, home, structure, strip mall, apartment complex, etc. Again, it is how you perceive what you are doing.

I believe that I take the most pride in the "service" aspect. As an investor, I feel like it is my responsibility to provide a solution to a homeowner in need of a solution, even if that solution isn't my option. I have told many sellers that, due to their situation, it is in their best interest to sell their home with a realtor. As an investor, you must look at the sellers as homeowners first and your personal/business gains are second. Now, of course, I am not in business to lose money. So, when I construct a deal with a seller, it must be a win-win.

Reputation is everything. My wife and I have made it our mission to treat people like our friends, to an extent. Again, this is still business. When you treat people with dignity and respect, they don't forget that. Due to our treating people the right way, we get about 20% of our new homes as referrals from previous sellers that we worked with 12-18 months ago. Remember, perception is reality. If you are perceived to be a slimy no good "investor," your business will suffer.

Unfortunately, depending on who you talk to, the word "investor" may have a negative connotation to it. That is because too many "investors" go into business for themselves and not to provide a service or product to the public. Once you make your business about helping other people, your company will grow faster than you could imagine.

SERVICE/PRODUCT

Treat your business as a living, breathing organism. Not literally, but don't assume that when you own 10-20 houses that you are set for life. The market always changes, and so do your customers. Understand that your customers are why your business is thriving and that you need them more than they need you. If you don't think so, then remove the customers from your company and see just how much money you make. There are many other home buyers in the area. Why should they work with you? What sets you apart?

What sets you apart is that you treat them like you need them. You provide win-win solutions. You care about your customers, and you care about their reviews. Excellent customer service is almost dead, with the exception of the Chick-Fillet restaurant franchise. Grant Cardone and Gary Vee have similar views when it comes to customer service. An unhappy customer is an opportunity to improve your service and your business. Granted, this isn't true 100% of the time. There are some sellers, tenants, and even buyers that will never be happy no matter what you do. When a legit complaint or situation arises, you make it right!

Chapter 9: Problem Solving

I believe in one of Gary Vaynerchuck's (Gary Vee) podcast; he talked about being a "firefighter." Meaning his responsibility is to put out fires or fix problems. If you look at the big picture, the more problems you can solve the more money you will make. My wife and I are constantly identifying issues within our business. We think, "how can we make our system more efficient, how can we cut back on this cost, how do we prevent this from happening next time, etc." We quickly realized that we must hire out and delegate responsibility.

By hiring and delegating, you not only give yourself back the time that you deserve, but you also have a professional and more experienced person that specializes in the area in which you are delegating or hiring. We first realized the need to hire a bookkeeper. Most people would ask, "Why would you pay someone for something that you can do yourself?". For me it's a no brainer. The bookkeeper knows the systems better and will do it the right way every time. I can spend a few hours a week inputting information and scanning documents, or I can pay to have it done while I'm taking care of other essential tasks.

The biggest problem that most small business owners have is their time management. When you have time, please read "The E-Myth" by Michael Gerber. The average small business owner wears every hat and works every position within the business. The owner is the accountant, handyman, marketing department, sales department, customer service representative, responsible for logistics and coordination, social media response team, etc. Mr. Gerber gets the point across that the business owner needs to work *"On"* the business instead of *"In"* the business.

Now let's change the focus from internal problems to problems that the homeowners may have. As I said before, the more problems that you can solve, the more money that you'll make overall. We get phone calls from sellers with issues that vary greatly. Some sellers went through a divorce, had a baby and need to upgrade to a new home, lost their job, got hired out of state, abruptly reassigned due to military orders, etc. I feel that it is my responsibility to help provide a solution to these homeowners. More often than not, I can offer them a win-win solution and in a timely manner. Depending on how long they have owned the home, how much is owed, and many other factors, I am able to provide them a solution that allows them to get out of a property and continue with that next phase in their life. Very few times have I not been able to offer a solution. In the case that I can not provide a solution within my business, I will refer them to another investor, or a realtor, that can assist them.

In the eyes of the seller, you must bend over backward. There have been times where I initially offered a solution to a seller, we couldn't come to an agreement, and that seller contacted me four months later and was very motivated to work a deal. Had I treated that seller wrong initially, they would have never thought of me and would have sent their business elsewhere.

Treat people right, and they'll always remember you. They'll tell their friends and family. They'll send referrals on Facebook and Instagram. Treat people wrong, and you have just begun the downfall of your business.

Chapter 10: Finances and Tracking

Unfortunately for most of us, we are not taught about finances in school. I believe this is a crime. I think about the hours and hours that I sat in high school and a few years of college, and terms like "Cash Flow," "Asset," "Liability," "Balance Sheet," "Debt to Income," "Loan to Value" and many more were never mentioned. The curriculum was dead set on making sure that we could do geometry, knew when the Ming Dynasty ended, and what the atomic weight of magnesium is.

This quick start guide is not designed to get too deep into finances. Depending on which investor, CPA, banker, or even financial advisor you speak with, you are liable to get different definitions of each. I like the way Rich Dad breaks down the definitions for the terms above. In my opinion, the most important thing that Rich Dad teaches is that an "Asset" makes you money and a "Liability" cost you money. Again, that is not taught in school. Most of us don't have one *Asset* to our name. We only have a ridiculous amount of *Liabilities*. We have car payments, mortgages, cell phone bills, and credit card debt to name a few. Even our kids are "Liabilities." Yes, that is right, your kid is a liability. If you don't have any Assets bringing in money each month, then you must work for a paycheck. Again, Rich Dad goes in depth with that concept in his book.

At a minimum, you must have a tracking system for your income, expenses, bills, debts, accounts receivable, etc. You can be stubborn and try to do it yourself with an excel spreadsheet, or you can automate your business with accounting software like QuickBooks. I have automated about 70% of our transactions through QuickBooks. 70% of the transactions are automatically attached to the right property or the right vendor. At any time, I can see which properties are my most profitable and which ones that I need to reassess. I can do this for a specific period, i.e., quarterly, monthly, annually, etc. QuickBooks is very user-friendly and is capable of so much more.

There are thousands of books written on finances. Choose wisely. I learned long ago to follow the teaching of the people who are where I want to be. I say this because a good majority of financial books out there tell us to get out of debt, to save, and invest in a 401K. They tell us that debt is bad, to live below our means, to save every penny that we can, that our homes are our most significant assets, etc. I tend to follow the advice of other entrepreneurs and real estate investors that have been successful in the same arena in which I wish to operate. I can't say it enough, *Rich Dad Poor Dad*, is a book that not just every investor should read, but every adult should read. That should be part of the curriculum in school because it has done more for me than "*Hamlet*" or "*The Iliad and the Odyssey*" has ever done for me as an adult.

At the end of this book is a recommended reading list of many books that I have found to be very valuable in both my growth as a person and as a businessman. I'm sure that those books probably cost me less than $300 and through the application of the principles in those books, the return on that investments in nearly infinite.

When it comes to finances and investing in general, most of us are very nearsighted, meaning we only see the upfront cost. We don't think long term. Stop that! That is not how the wealthy people of the world think. I know some entrepreneurs that pay thousands of dollars a year to go to seminars. We may think that is ridiculous. It isn't. If I spend $5,000 to learn something that will make me $50,000 or maybe even $5,000,000, that is a win all day long. So, when it comes to finances, you must forget everything you learned growing up with a consumer mindset. Learn to be an investor. Learn to think like an investor. Moreover, learn to evaluate short term and long term returns like an investor.

Chapter 11-Asset Protection

This chapter is written to make you think long term. This is to provide information and should not be considered as advice. I highly recommend speaking with your CPA and local real estate attorney when choosing the best structure and protection for your business.

When new investors begin buying, selling, flipping, or even landlording, they typically don't think about the long term investment and long term risk associated with doing a high volume of transactions. They think about the next purchase or the next deal. We teach our clients to build their business like they are going to have millions. Unfortunately, if you have millions that also means that you have millions to lose. I read a statistic that said 94% of the worldwide lawsuits are filed here in the U.S. Statistically speaking, at some point in your investing career, you may face some litigation, regardless of merit.

I was taught early on to set up the business to protect it from frivolous lawsuits. Keep in mind that **anyone can sue anyone for anything in the U.S**. That being said, you want to protect your assets so that the judge, or whoever, throws out the case and awards you the attorney fees. You want to make your business an unattractive target for opposing attorneys to file a lawsuit. At the end of the day, if an attorney can't get paid, they are less likely to take the case and come after your business.

There are many ways that you can set up your business, and I'll cover a few.

1) LLC/S-Corp - As I mentioned in the beginning few chapters, there are different types of entities. Entities are essential because the entity is separate from the investor. The investor owns the entity, but the investor is not the entity. For example, John Smith starts up Smith Homes, LLC. Let's say that Smith Homes, LLC. buys a property at 123 Main St. John Smith doesn't own the property, but his business does.

Therefore, in most cases, any issues or concerns with 123 Main St. are the concern of Smith Homes, LLC. and not directly of John Smith.

The separation of person and entity is crucial for so many reasons. In the example above, if a person wanted to sue Smith Homes, LLC., because of a slip and fall at 123 Main St., John Smith and his personal assets should be protected and should not be part of any litigation. However, if John Smith had bought the home in his name and not in an entity, then John Smith and all his personal assets may be at risk.

2) <u>Trusts</u> - I've spoken with many attorneys and, depending on their specialty, they may or may not understand the legal protection that a trust offers. Anyone, not just an investor, can use a trust. In real estate, a trust is often used as an estate planning tool. A trust is usually comprised of 3 parties: Trustor, Trustee, and Beneficiary. Please consult your attorney for further details on the roles and responsibilities of each.

Many investors will put each of their properties in a trust, or each property may be placed into their own separate trust. Many investors will put their entities in a trust. Many investors may put their personal assets in a trust. There are options and reasons behind doing so. Again, consult your attorney.

3) <u>Umbrella Insurance Policy</u> - Some investors, to simplify their processes, accounting, etc., will purchase all their properties and run their business through their names. Yes, they are at risk; however, they will take out a large umbrella insurance policy that is valued at more than the sum of their properties. For example, John Smith owns 20 houses free and clear that are valued at $4,000,000. The investor may take out an umbrella insurance policy of $6,000,000 to cover the investment assets and his personal and family assets.

These are just three strategies that are commonly used. An investor may use a combination of the three. Keep in mind that each offers different protection and may have different tax implications. For more in-depth information on asset protection, I highly recommend reading, "*A Practical Guide to Asset Protection*" by Bud Lethbridge, Blair Jackson, M.A., J.D., and G. James Christiansen, J.D. I met Mr. Lethbridge in Utah. His research and attention to detail were more than impressive. He owns a company called Veil Corporate in Utah that anyone can call for more information and assistance.

Chapter 12-Fear is Fake

Realize right now that you are going to make mistakes. No matter what books you read, what courses you take, or what mentors you have holding your hand, you are going to make mistakes. There are two ways to deal with mistakes; they can defeat you, or they can propel you forward. You can be defeated and sulk and think that it wasn't meant to be. Or, you can take the mistakes and turn them into a learning point, a valuable lesson that you'll never repeat, even a reason to look at the same situation differently. You are going to learn more from mistakes and losses than you are from the victories.

We began with the grand idea of flipping houses. My first flip was an absolute disaster. I did everything that an investor is not supposed to do. I paid too much for the property, I didn't have my contractor sign specific documentation prior to beginning the project, I used materials that were too expensive for the neighborhood, the home was overpriced, and it sat on the market for five months. I made $0 on my very first flip. I began to question everything. Do I have what it takes? Am I smart enough to be successful in real estate? Is this for me?

I regret to admit that I took a few months off before getting back to aggressively searching for my next house to flip. The second flip was the dream flip. It took only 92 days from purchase, to rehab, to sold. We made a quick net profit of $22,000 without using our own money. I took this opportunity not to repeat the bad things I did with the first house. I bought it at the right price, the contractor signed all of the documents before we began the project, and the realtor listed the home at the right price to get it sold fast. I was on cloud nine.

Then, with the third house we flipped, we didn't have the same results. We purchased the home at the end of October. The contractors were running behind because of the winter weather. What should have taken three weeks took about seven weeks to rehab. Then the house hit the market in the middle of January. Again, lousy weather usually slows down the real estate activity in our area. We kept getting inquiries from people wanting to rent the home, but not to buy it. We decided to rent the home in March. We quickly realized that our mortgage was only about $350, and we were receiving $950 for rent giving us a positive cash flow of $600 a month. That was March of 2016. A few months later, we developed a system to purchase homes, "Subject To", as I described in an earlier chapter.

We began acquiring homes like wildfire. We went from having two houses as rentals, to seven houses, to eleven houses, then to fifteen houses. Were we scared? YES, at first. We quickly realized that we are now responsible for so many mortgages every single month. No pressure, right? Like the title of this chapter, Fear is Fake. Instead of being scared and asking ourselves, "what are we going to do about all of these mortgages," we immersed ourselves in learning the art of landlording.

The task of being in the army and trying to manage all these houses was getting out of hand. Realizing that our passive income with the rentals would bring us more money than my wife's job, we decided that my wife quit her job to focus on our business. That is when we really took off. My wife got into the books and learned about rentals, contracts, legalities, policies, etc. That freed me up to focus on acquiring the next house, then the next one, and so on.

We could have been scared and handed the houses off to another investor in fear of not being able to service all the properties. We rose to the occasion and took the stance that it was our responsibility to figure it out. It was on us to learn fast, to take our losses, and to get better with each new acquisition and each new tenant. Our rental agreement went from being eight pages to fourteen pages. That is because any time a tenant finds a loophole or gets one over on us, we add a clause into our contract to prevent that from ever happening again.

Success is scary. That isn't a misprint. Success is scary. We are nowhere close to reaching our potential, but when we think of owning 100, 200, or even 1000 rental properties, that can be scary. I welcome the challenge. More properties mean more problems, more issues, more responsibility, more mortgages, more people relying on us, etc. With systems, structure, and a great team, that can and will be very profitable.

A person won't risk the chance of prosperity for fear of losing. You won't risk leaving your job to start your real estate business for fear of not being able to pay your bills. That is a very understandable fear. You don't have to quit your job tomorrow to begin your business. You start your business while you are working your current job. You grind through the long days and late nights creating your company and your brand. You talk to buyers, sellers, contractors, etc. to get out there and to conduct business in your area. It may take a few months, or even a few years, before your company makes the same amount, or more, income than your job does. At that point…QUIT your JOB! Work for yourself. Build your business and your legacy. Don't let fear stop this from happening. Go and do it!

Chapter 13-Take Action

Knowledge without action is pointless. Some people go to seminar after seminar to hear about the same topic. They'll sit in the audience nodding their heads and agreeing with everything the speaker is saying. They love the idea of passive income, financial freedom, and owning assets. As soon as the speaker says that there is a cost for their program, their expertise, and their time, the attendee immediately changes their tone.

I have personally experienced this many times before. People want great results without putting in the work, taking the risk, missing some of the parties, or putting out signs and building a website instead of watching football all weekend. There is no substitute for effort and hard work. No one is going to lay the groundwork for your success.

Knowledge and experience usually are not free. You will have to invest some of your time and money in learning from the trials and tribulations of people who are successful in the arena in which you begin your business. You don't have to break the bank. Books on Amazon.com generally cost less than $15. That is a meager price to pay for tips, techniques, procedures, guidelines, and 1st hand accounts on how to be successful in the field that you choose.

Grant Cardone says, "start now." Don't wait to have all the answers and everything figured out. Grant says to "Commit now and figure out the details on the way." I agree with that philosophy. If a person waits for the perfect opportunity, they'll starve. Life will never be perfect. The deal will never be perfect. The time will never be perfect. There are always more reasons and excuses not to do something than there are to actually do it. So, make a commitment to yourself and go with it.

We all want to quit our jobs and work for ourselves. We all want to control our time and fate. We all want to have the means to travel more. We all have dreams that the typical 9-5 job won't allow us to achieve. Stop following the crowd and create your path.

My wife and I have recently opened our own real estate business consulting firm in which we are blessed to be able to help new investors, both local and through distance learning, start their real estate investing businesses. It is gratifying to watch people turn an idea into a reality. Real estate is not a "get rich quick" scheme. We walk our clients from day one, through marketing, negotiating, through closing on houses, scheduling and overseeing repairs, qualifying their tenants, and into becoming a landlord. For more information on our 1-on-1 "1st Step" business coaching, contact me directly at Adam@1stStepLLC.com for a FREE CONSULTATION.

Do something. Don't look back in 5-10 years and wish you had started. Do it now. You can make more money; you can't make more time. Think Big! Take Action! And remember, "There is no growth in your comfort zone."

Recommend Reading List

In no particular order:

MINDSET

RICH DAD POOR DAD
-Robert Kiyosaki

CASH FLOW QUADRANT
-Robert Kiyosaki

THE 10X RULE
-Grant Cardone

THINK AND GROW RICH
-Napoleon Hill

THE E-MYTH REVISITED
-Michael Gerber

THE FOUR HOUR WORK WEEK
-Timothy Ferris

HOW TO WIN FRIENDS AND INFLUENCE PEOPLE
-Dale Carnegie

INVESTING

INVESTING IN REAL ESTATE WITH LEASE OPTIONS AND "SUBJECT-TO" DEALS
-Wendy Patton

THE BOOK ON TAX STRATEGIES FOR THE SAVY REAL ESTATE INVESTOR
-Amanda Han and Matthew MacFarland

THE BOOK ON INVESTING IN REAL ESTATE WITH NO AND LOW MONEY DOWN
-Brandon Turner

THE BOOK ON RENTAL PROPERTY INVESTING
-Brandon Turner

THE BOOK ON MANAGING RENTAL PROPERTIES
-Brandon and Heather Turner

SALES

SALE OR BE SOLD
-Grant Cardone

THE SECRETS OF CLOSING THE SALE

-Zig Ziglar

SELLING 101

-Zig Ziglar

www.ingramcontent.com/pod-product-compliance
Lightning Source LLC
Chambersburg PA
CBHW051323220526
45468CB00004B/1473